EMPOWERING
CAMPUS MINISTRY

a condensed version of

Empowered by the Spirit

COMMITTEE ON EDUCATION
UNITED STATES CONFERENCE OF CATHOLIC BISHOPS

United States Conference of Catholic Bishops
Washington, D.C.

The document *Empowering Campus Ministry: A Condensed Version of "Empowered by the Spirit"* was developed as a resource by the Committee on Education of the United States Conference of Catholic Bishops (USCCB). It was reviewed by the committee chairman, Bishop Donald W. Wuerl, and has been authorized for publication by the undersigned.

Msgr. William P. Fay, *General Secretary, USCCB*

To obtain copies of *Empowered by the Spirit: Campus Ministry Faces the Future*—the U.S. Catholic bishops' pastoral letter on which this resource is based— contact USCCB Publishing at 800-235-8722.

Photo credits: p. 1, CNS photo by Karen Callaway; p. 3, CNS photo by Tom Tracy; p. 4, CNS photo by Amy Buck; p. 5, CNS photo by Owen Sweeney III; pp. 6, 7, 9, 11, 12, photos by Robert J. Downs; p. 8, photo by Michael Galligan-Stierle; p. 13, CNS photo by Fred LeBlanc.

First Printing, October 2002

ISBN 1-57455-497-2

INTRODUCTION

F or over a century, Catholic campus ministry in our country has been forming communities of faith that witness to the presence of the risen Christ. Now we are at the beginning of a new era filled with challenging opportunities to build up the faith community on campuses and to promote the well-being of higher education and society. This new era challenges campus ministry to respond creatively to the promptings of the Spirit for the good of the Church. We offer prayerful support, encouragement, and guidance to the men and women who are committed to bring Christ's message to the academic world. We have consulted with many of them. Their suggestions affirmed that all who minister in higher education have common concerns and desires for cooperation. Many perspectives and suggestions here should help those who serve so well. In our 1985 pastoral

letter *Empowered by the Spirit*—on which this resource is based—we turned our attention primarily to the ministry of the Church on these public and private campuses, where millions of Catholics are prepared as future leaders of society and the Church.

I. HISTORY AND CURRENT OPPORTUNITIES

The Church's response to this new era benefits from an awareness of the history of the Newman Movement in the United States, a lay initiative that began in 1883. Farsighted leaders, recognizing that the growing number of Catholics attending public institutions needed support and instruction in their religious heritage, responded by establishing clubs for Catholic students. The second stage began with the 1908 establishment of the first association of Catholic clubs in state universities. This phase was characterized by a defensive attitude of some Catholic students and chaplains toward the academic world, while others decried the lack of support from the church hierarchy.

In the third stage, beginning after Vatican II and continuing until the present, the Church has grown in appreciation and support of campus ministry. We endorse the improving relationship between the Church on campus and the academic community. We affirm the development of ecumenical relationships and give full support to more creative efforts in this direction. A remarkable diversity of legitimate approaches to campus ministry has developed to match available resources with the unique situations at particular institutions. Catholics are attending colleges and universities in numbers far exceeding their percentage of the general population. We encourage Catholics on campus to contribute their insights and values to the important debate over how to improve the quality of higher education in our country, and we challenge faculty, staff, and students to contribute time and talents to help both the academic community and the Church.

II. CAMPUS MINISTRY AND THE RELATIONSHIP BETWEEN THE CHURCH AND HIGHER EDUCATION

C ampus ministry is an expression of the Church's special desire to be present to all involved in higher education, reflecting the Church's long history of cultivating the intellectual life. However, modern government has increasingly assumed responsibility for higher education, resulting in a split between the Church and the university, with a good deal of mutual misunderstanding. The time has come to forge a new relationship that respects the unique character of each, for society's well-being relies upon the integration of faith and reason.

We respect the autonomy of the academic community and appreciate its great contributions to the common social good: expanding our knowledge, teaching critical thinking and the search for truth, and providing skills for productive, harmonious, and responsible living. The Church likewise benefits from these contributions, which help

Christians to deepen and articulate their faith. It is vital that campus ministry maintain a fundamental appreciation of higher education's contributions to society and the Church.

The Church contributes its mission to preach the Gospel and seeks to work with higher education toward the mutual goal of developing a culture in which human beings can realize their full potential. The faith community and higher education are involved in a common pursuit of the life of wisdom. The Church brings its traditional understanding of wisdom: the highest principles that integrate all knowledge, the deepest secrets of human nature, and a personal synthesis that unites knowledge and love. For Christians, this pursuit finds fulfillment in Jesus Christ, the wisdom of God who reveals the mystery of human existence.

Campus ministry can be defined as the public presence and service through which properly prepared baptized persons are empowered by the Spirit to use their gifts on behalf of the Church in order to be signs and instruments of the kingdom in the academic world. Creativity has produced great diversity in approach, as campus ministers strive to form a searching, believing, loving, worshiping Catholic presence on campus. For these reasons, then, the eye of faith discerns campus ministry where commitment to Christ and care for the academic world meet in purposeful activity to serve and realize the Kingdom of God.

III. PERSONS WHO SERVE ON CAMPUS

The Church carries out its pastoral mission to the academic world through both its communal life and the Christian witness of individuals. By virtue of the universal priesthood of baptism, all the faithful of the academic community have the opportunity and the obligation, according to their gifts, to help higher education achieve its potential and to build up the Church on campus. We hope that students, faculty, staff, and administrators act upon their unique opportunity and calling to lead and direct campus ministry programs, according to their gifts. These individuals are particularly needed on the many campuses where no campus ministry programs exist.

Professional campus ministers—lay, religious, and ordained; men and women—are called upon to provide vision and overall direction to the well-being of the academic community and the Church on campus. We encourage campus ministers to prepare for  the challenges of their position by taking responsibility for their own personal and professional development. We likewise encourage the formation of team ministries. We recognize our responsibility as bishops to offer all campus ministers moral support, to provide financial assistance, to help them achieve competency, and to provide the support of the diocesan director of campus ministry.

IV. ASPECTS OF CAMPUS MINISTRY

Six ministerial functions reflect the Church's general mission on campus and the distinctive situation of higher education today.

1. Forming the Faith Community
2. Appropriating the Faith
3. Forming the Christian Conscience
4. Educating for Justice
5. Facilitating Personal Development
6. Developing Leaders for the Future

1. Forming the Faith Community

Campus ministry forms faith communities in an academic environment that knows solidarity but also alienation. The call to form communities of faith flows from this pastoral situation as well as the example of  Christ and his followers. The Church gains credibility when the dream of community produces genuine commitment and intelligent effort. The baptized who experience acceptance, healing, and empowerment in the faith community can bring an understanding ear, a reconciling touch, and an encouraging voice to alienated persons on campus.

Warm, welcoming campus ministry leaders can gain the active involvement of the campus community. The ministry of presence, in which leaders of the faith community participate in campus life, initiates contact with potential members and enhances existing relationships— showing appreciation that attracts students, faculty, and staff to participate in the faith community. Celebrating the Eucharist is a powerful means of building this faith community, just as Jesus Christ did when, led by the Spirit, he gathered a community of followers. In Mass and communion services, flexibility, broad use of legitimate liturgical options, and homilies that realistically apply the Gospel can enhance the inherent community-building power of the Eucharist while respecting the sensibilities of the academic community.

2. Appropriating the Faith

Campus ministry has a special responsibility to enable Catholics to achieve a more adult appropriation of their faith so that they can live in greater communion with God and his Church, give more effective witness to the Gospel, and face the challenges to belief that exist in the academic world. Campus life tends to reinforce these intellectual and social challenges, which are intensified by the general religious illiteracy in our culture.

To respond credibly, intelligently, and sensitively to honest inquiry requires careful preparation. All the members of the community of faith have a right to theological education that prepares them to meet this responsibility by keeping alive the great questions of meaning, purpose, and identity and by providing a coherent vision of life that serves as a unifying principle for all learning. Effective strategies must create a climate in which theological learning is respected, must deal realistically with the situations of the targeted audiences, and must work with others in the academic community to improve the response of higher education to the problem of religious illiteracy.

3. Forming the Christian Conscience

Many questions of personal values and ethics inevitably arise for individuals in the academic community. As they deal with these questions, they come under the influence of the campus's moral climate, which includes high idealism and unselfish commitment as well as moral relativism and selfish indi-

vidualism. Campus ministry has the crucial task of assisting in the formation of Catholic consciences, which involves a transforming renewal of mind in accord with the will of God. This divine summons must be answered freely and intelligently; but when genuine virtue is acquired, then good actions flow more spontaneously, and new strength is found to live according to one's ideals.

Campus ministry can help to form consciences through personal encounters, homilies, seminars, and peer ministry. Campus ministers must be—and *be perceived* to be—in touch with the texture and complexities of the moral problems generated by campus life. They must also have a working knowledge of the wisdom found in the Catholic traditions on particular moral questions. An open atmosphere is needed so that community members can speak freely about the prevailing campus attitudes and pressures, as well as their own outlooks and decision making.

4. Educating for Justice

Most agree that higher education makes a valuable contribution by providing a forum to discuss questions of social justice in a civil and reasoned fashion so that constructive solutions can be worked out. But alongside striking examples of personal commitment to justice, we sense strong currents of individualism and apathy that undercut concern for the common good and eclipse the urgency of social concerns. Campus ministry is called to be a consistent and vigorous advocate for justice, peace, and reverence for all life. With this in mind, campus ministers have the responsibility of keeping alive the vision of the Church on campus as a servant dedicated to works of justice.

We call special attention to the need to teach and learn the coherent body of Catholic social thought (see box below). This education for justice can be carried out in a variety of ways, but it is enhanced by including an action component, such as service project opportunities, paired with systematic reflection on those experiences. Some issues call for more public response by the Church on campus, and the faith community can touch the conscience of the academic world by sponsoring campus programs designed to raise consciousness.

Seven Principles of Catholic Social Teaching

In their 1991 statement *A Century of Social Teaching* and their 1998 reflection *Sharing Catholic Social Teaching*, the U.S. Catholic bishops identified seven key principles of Catholic social teaching that have been developed in a century of Vatican and episcopal documents:

1. Life and dignity of the human person
2. Call to family, community, and participation
3. Rights and responsibilities
4. Option for and with the poor and vulnerable
5. Dignity of work and the rights of workers
6. Solidarity
7. Care for God's creation

These key principles have been explored in many subsequent resources developed for a variety of audiences by the United States Conference of Catholic Bishops.

5. Facilitating Personal Development

Many find academia to be an ideal setting filled with rich opportunities for establishing identities, forming relationships, discerning vocations, and charting the direction of their lives. On the other hand, this vast potential for self-fulfillment is often ignored, impeded, or interpreted exclusively in terms of career and material success. Critics generally agree that reform is needed—in institutional goals, curricula, and student involvement—so that higher education can achieve its proper goal of facilitating the full personal development of students. Campus ministry must be attuned to these voices of reform, and it must be prepared to function as the ally of genuine personal development. When campus ministry brings the light of the Gospel to the educational process, the search for personal development leads to a Christian humanism that fuses the positive values and meanings in the culture with the light of faith.

Campus ministry can facilitate personal growth through vibrant sacramental life, pastoral counseling, courses, seminars, and retreats that enable Catholics on campus to integrate their collegiate experience with their Christian faith. This important work is enhanced when ministers are perceived as persons of prayer who are serious about their own growth; when members of the faithful have opportunities for more personal contact; and when individuals assist their institutions in educating whole persons for lifelong growth and responsible citizenship.

6. Developing Leaders for the Future

Campus ministry has the great opportunity to tap the immense pool of talent (students, staff, and faculty) in our colleges and universities and to help form leaders for both society and the Church. The clear teaching of Scripture is that gifts and talents are not given simply for personal advantage; they are to be used generously and appropriately for the benefit of others. Vatican II, recognizing this potential, called on all adult Christians to prepare themselves for this task. Effective contemporary leadership is connected with a sense of loving service and a more mature self-knowledge. The nature of Christian leadership can also be viewed as a vocation we all receive from God.

Campus ministers can facilitate leader formation by encouraging the faithful to identify their gifts and to use them for the common good. Individuals must be helped to gain confidence in their abilities; they need proper training and opportunities to improve their leadership skills, including involvement in campus groups and activities. In addition, students must be helped to discern and prepare for their vocations in life. Campus ministers also need to establish personal contact with faculty and administrators to foster their leadership in the faith community. And the local church should make every effort to train individuals to carry out campus ministry on campuses where there are no professional ministerial personnel.

EPILOGUE

We are convinced that campus ministry is vital to the future of Church and society. We know it is important to find dedicated persons for this ministry who have solid faith, a love for the academic world, and the ability to relate well to both students and faculty. They need proper training, including personal development, practical experience, and theological study. Advanced degrees help to gain credibility in the academic world. We are committed to providing the best professional campus ministers possible and intend to hold them accountable for dedicated and creative service to the academic community. Our responsibilities extend to ensuring that within each diocese, adequate funding is available for campus ministry, with an overall plan for allocating resources. Our hope is that this letter will mark the beginning of a new phase in Catholic campus ministry in the United States. In our vision, campus ministry, empowered by the Spirit, faces a future bright with promise.

NOTES